Editor in Chief: Ana Doblado
Original Spanish Text: A-rredondo / Susaeta editorial team
Book Design and Illustrations: A-rredondo
Production: Antonia Maria Martinez
Art Editor: José de Haro

ISBN: 978-0-7097-1775-1

Design and illustrations
A-rredondo

English edition translated from
the Spanish and edited by
Maureen Spurgeon

The HUMAN BODY

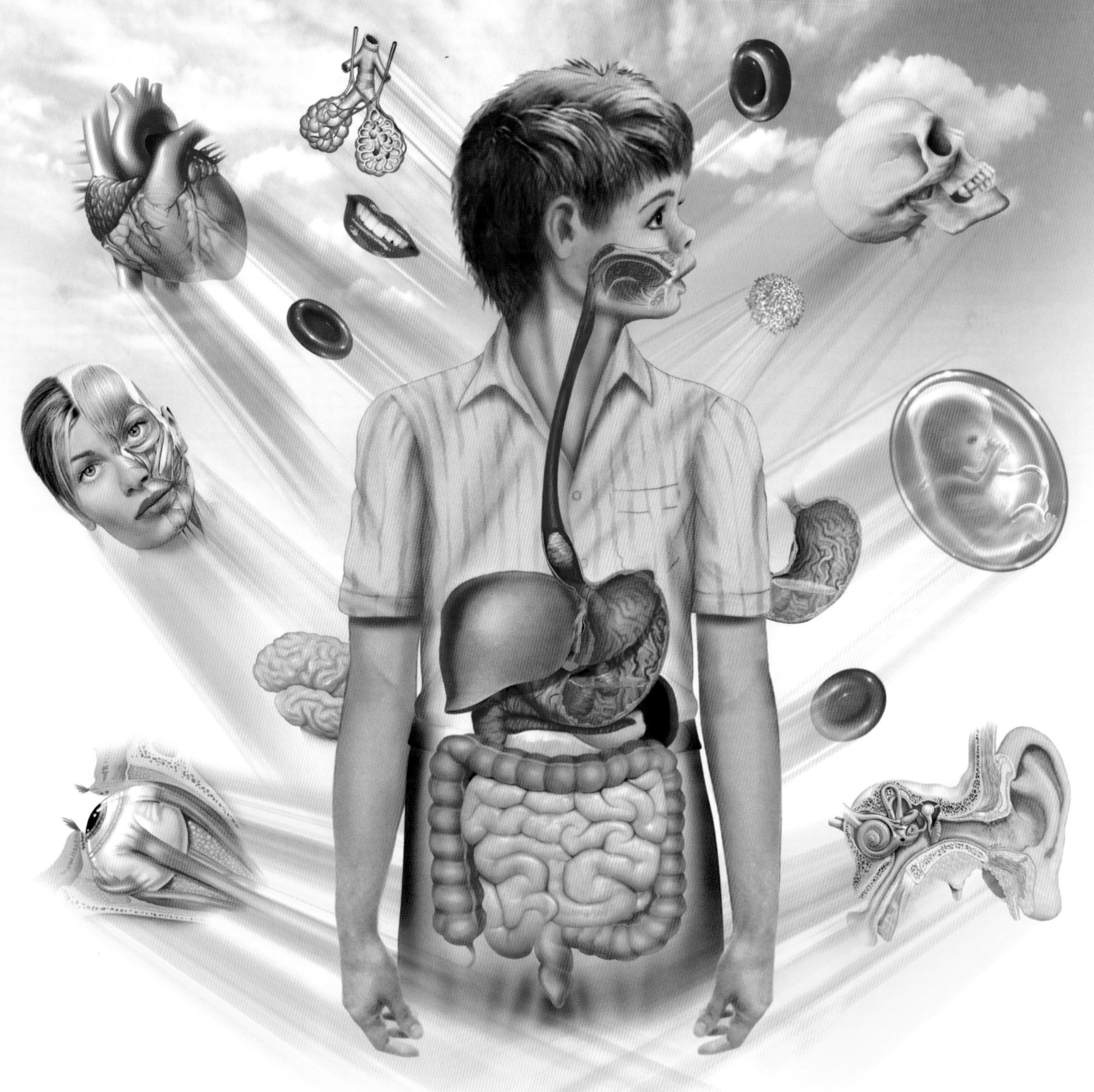

Brown Watson

Around the Human Body

Can you imagine being really small? Small enough to go inside the human body and find your own way around? Well, this is your chance! Come along and discover the parts of your body and how they work.

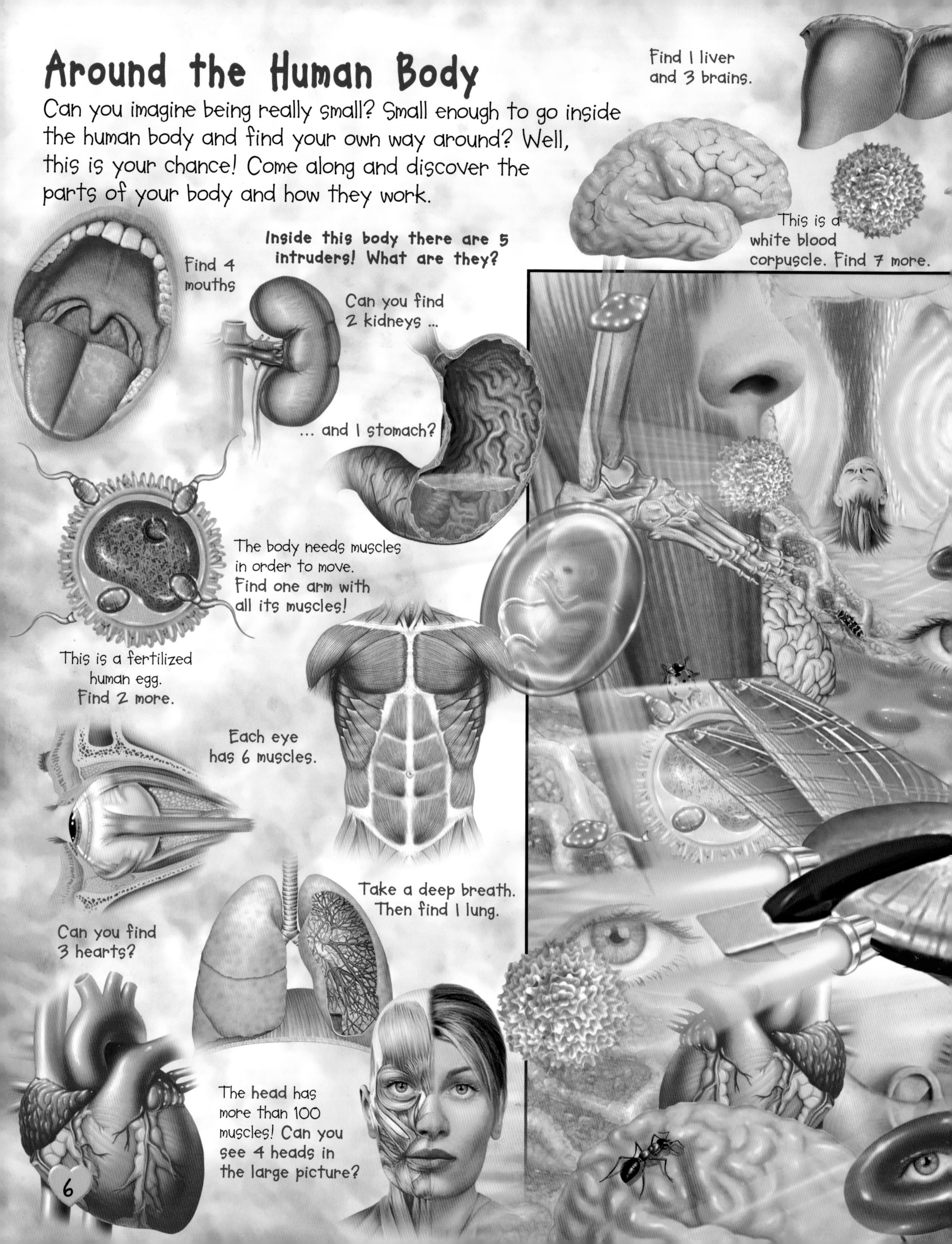

Find 1 liver and 3 brains.
This is a white blood corpuscle. Find 7 more.
Inside this body there are 5 intruders! What are they?
Find 4 mouths
Can you find 2 kidneys ...
... and 1 stomach?
The body needs muscles in order to move. Find one arm with all its muscles!
This is a fertilized human egg. Find 2 more.
Each eye has 6 muscles.
Take a deep breath. Then find 1 lung.
Can you find 3 hearts?
The head has more than 100 muscles! Can you see 4 heads in the large picture?

Find 6 sections of the skeleton.
There are 8 red blood corpuscles like this one to be found.
Find 5 blood platelets.
There are 5 foetuses (developing babies) to find.
Can you see 3 ears?
See if you can find 3 noses!
There are 2 expectant mothers to find.

The brain and the spinal column

The brain is the most delicate, fragile and complex part of the human body. So, it is well protected! Although it weighs only 1.4 kg in an adult, it is a perfect database. The brain is made up of 100,000 million cells, more than the number of stars in the Milky Way.

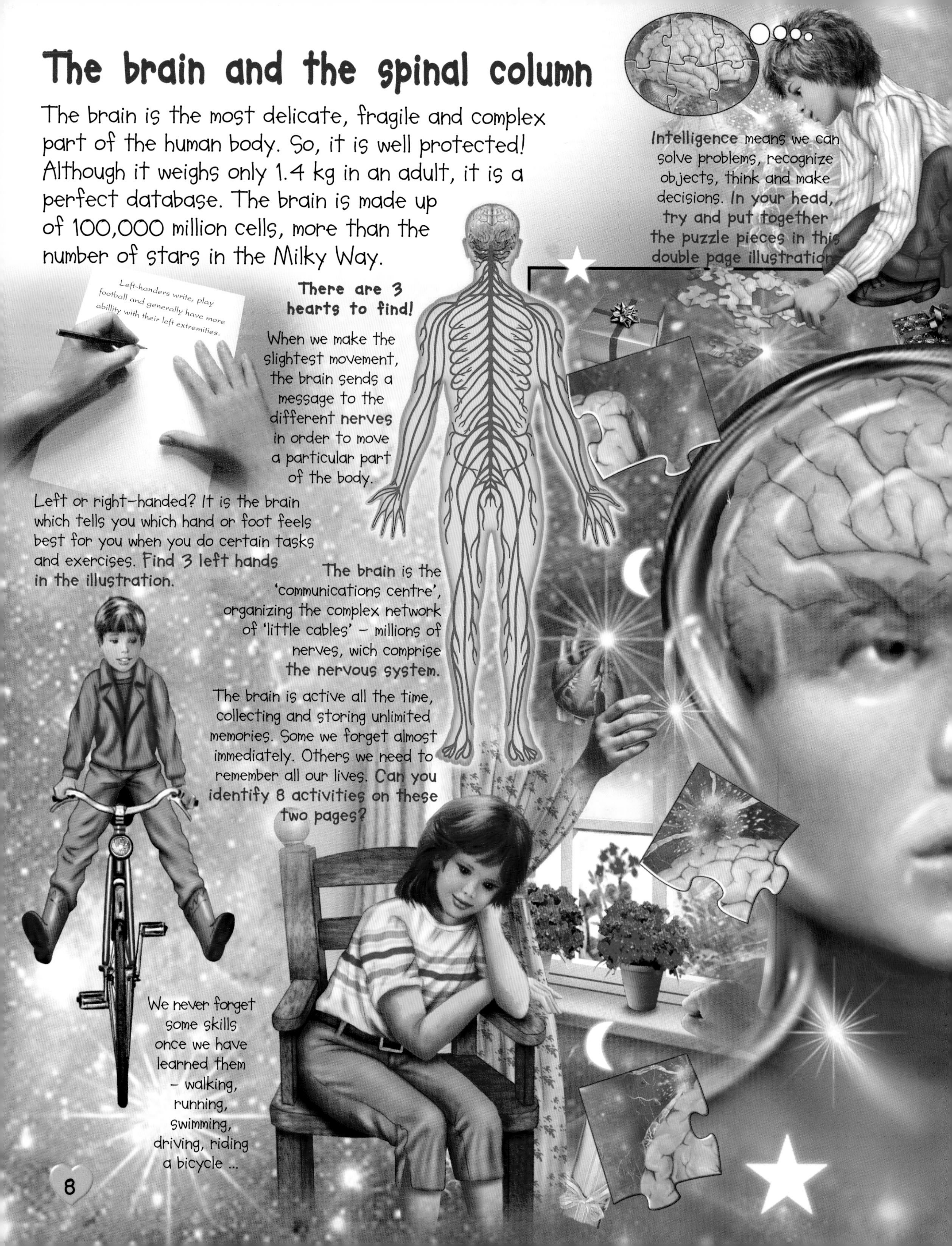

Left-handers write, play football and generally have more abillity with their left extremities.

Intelligence means we can solve problems, recognize objects, think and make decisions. **In your head, try and put together the puzzle pieces in this double page illustration.**

There are 3 hearts to find!

When we make the slightest movement, the brain sends a message to the different **nerves** in order to move a particular part of the body.

Left or right-handed? It is the brain which tells you which hand or foot feels best for you when you do certain tasks and exercises. **Find 3 left hands in the illustration.**

The brain is the 'communications centre', organizing the complex network of 'little cables' – millions of nerves, wich comprise **the nervous system.**

The brain is active all the time, collecting and storing unlimited memories. Some we forget almost immediately. Others we need to remember all our lives. **Can you identify 8 activities on these two pages?**

We never forget some skills once we have learned them – walking, running, swimming, driving, riding a bicycle ...

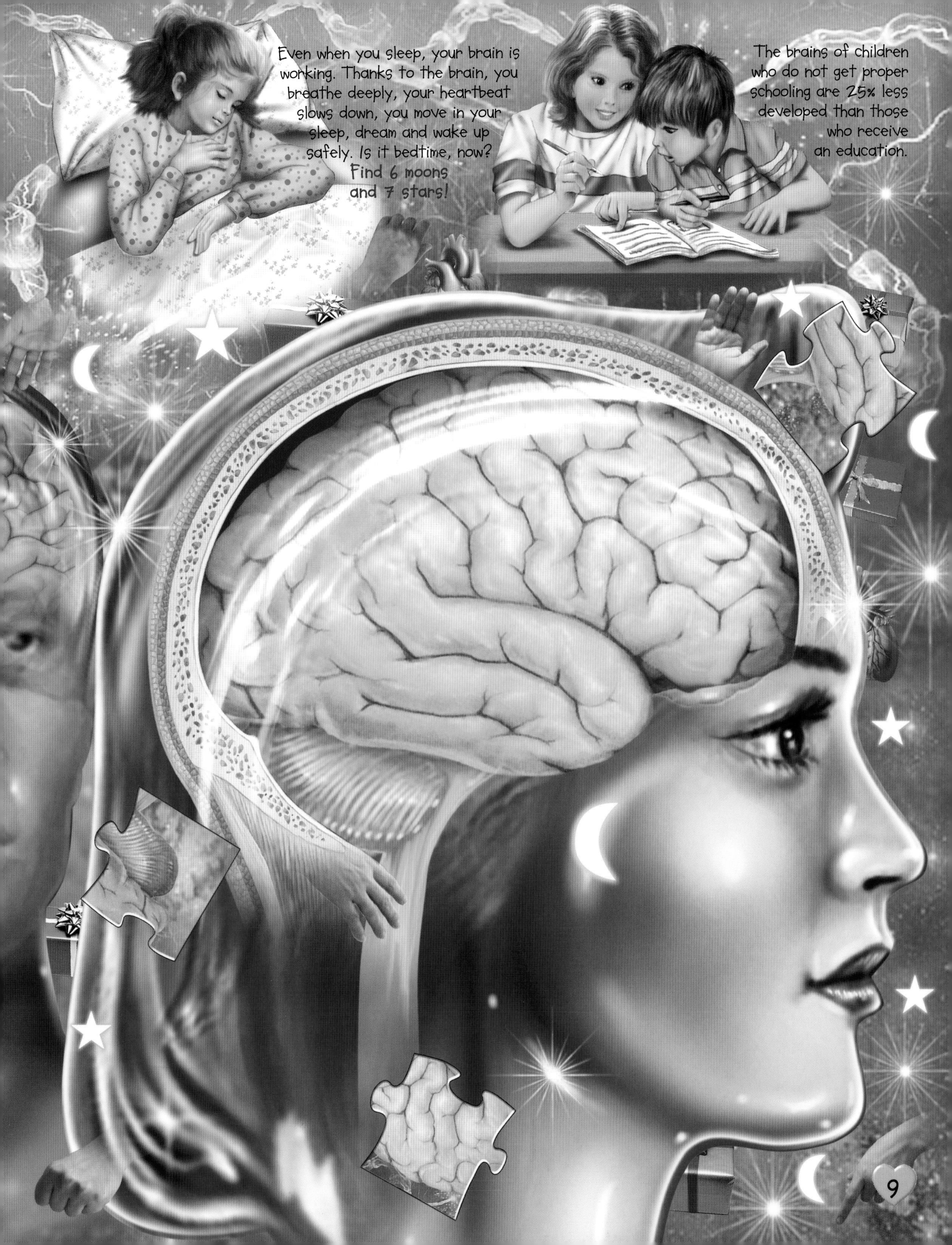
Even when you sleep, your brain is working. Thanks to the brain, you breathe deeply, your heartbeat slows down, you move in your sleep, dream and wake up safely. Is it bedtime, now?
Find 6 moons and 7 stars!
The brains of children who do not get proper schooling are 25% less developed than those who receive an education.

The five senses

The five senses are – sight, taste, hearing, smell and touch. These enable us to see beautiful things, to enjoy food, to listen to music, to smell flowers and to recognize different textures and surfaces.

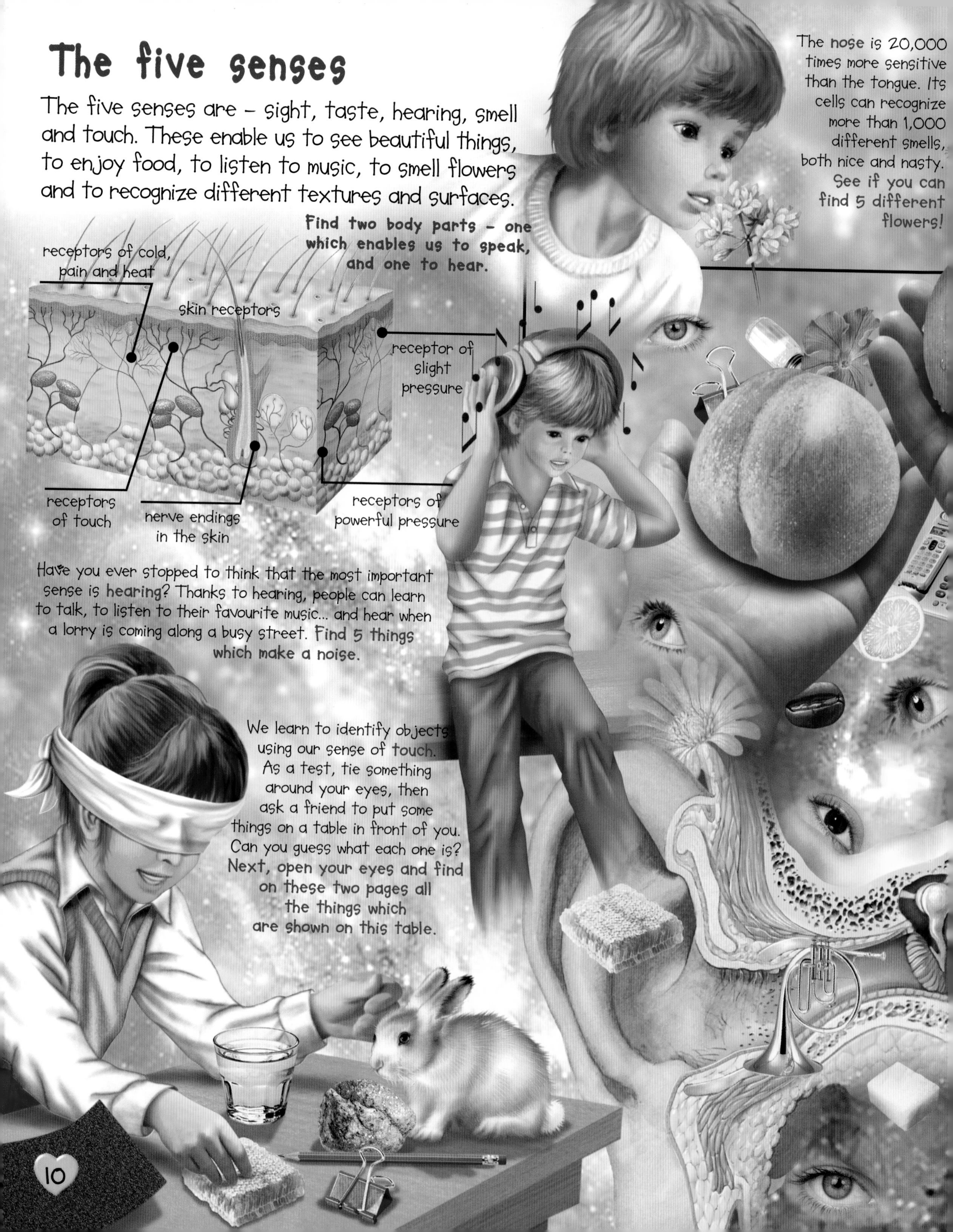

Find two body parts – one which enables us to speak, and one to hear.

The **nose** is 20,000 times more sensitive than the tongue. Its cells can recognize more than 1,000 different smells, both nice and nasty. **See if you can find 5 different flowers!**

Have you ever stopped to think that the most important sense is **hearing**? Thanks to hearing, people can learn to talk, to listen to their favourite music... and hear when a lorry is coming along a busy street. **Find 5 things which make a noise.**

We learn to identify objects using our sense of **touch**. As a test, tie something around your eyes, then ask a friend to put some things on a table in front of you. Can you guess what each one is? **Next, open your eyes and find on these two pages all the things which are shown on this table.**

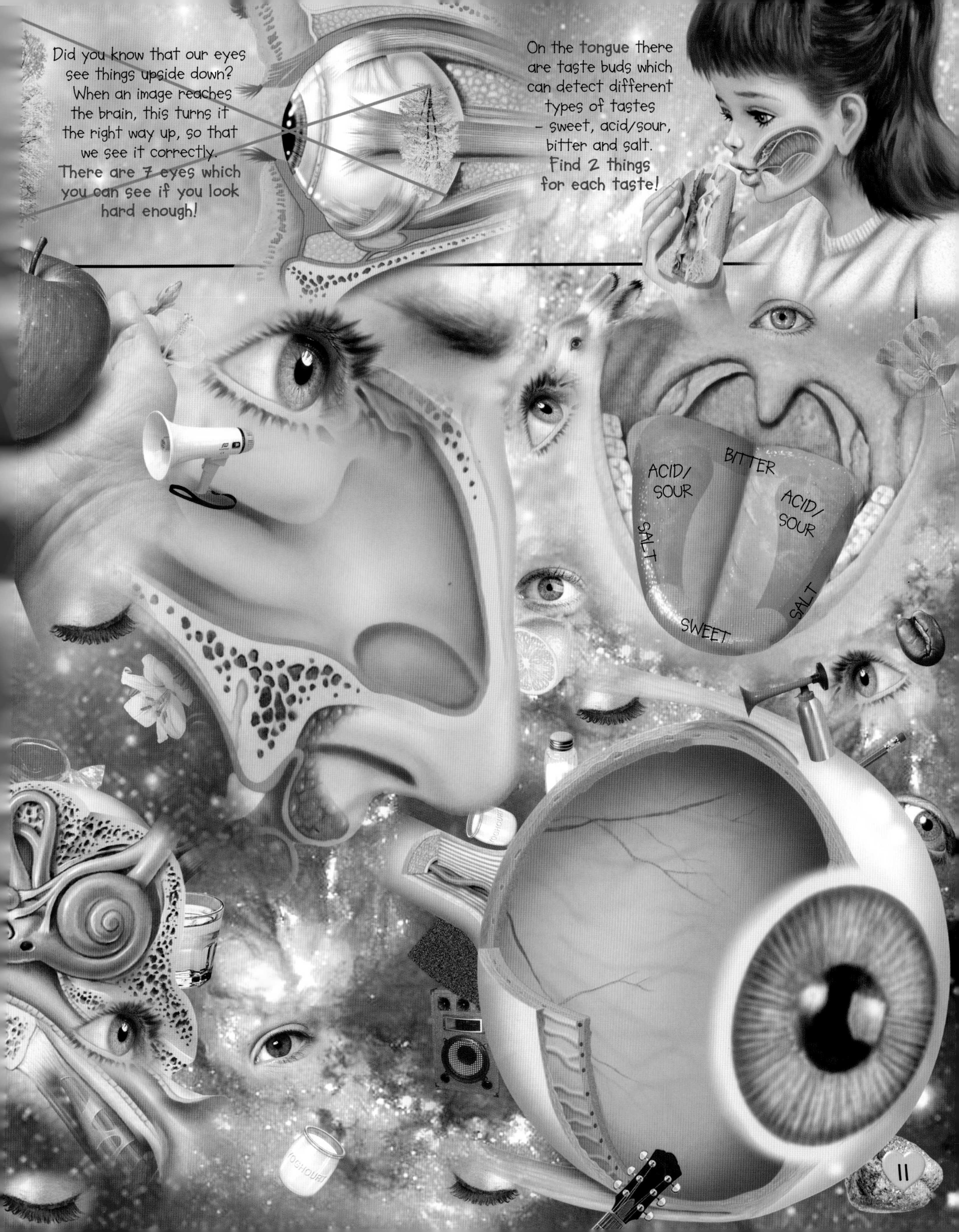
Did you know that our eyes see things upside down? When an image reaches the brain, this turns it the right way up, so that we see it correctly. There are 7 eyes which you can see if you look hard enough!
On the tongue there are taste buds which can detect different types of tastes – sweet, acid/sour, bitter and salt. Find 2 things for each taste!
BITTER
ACID/ SOUR
ACID/ SOUR
SALT
SALT
SWEET
YOGHOURT
YOGHOURT

The heart and the blood

Blood flows through the veins and the arteries, carrying oxygen and nourishing all parts of the body. In the lungs the blood is enriched with oxygen. The heart then pumps this oxygenated blood around the body.

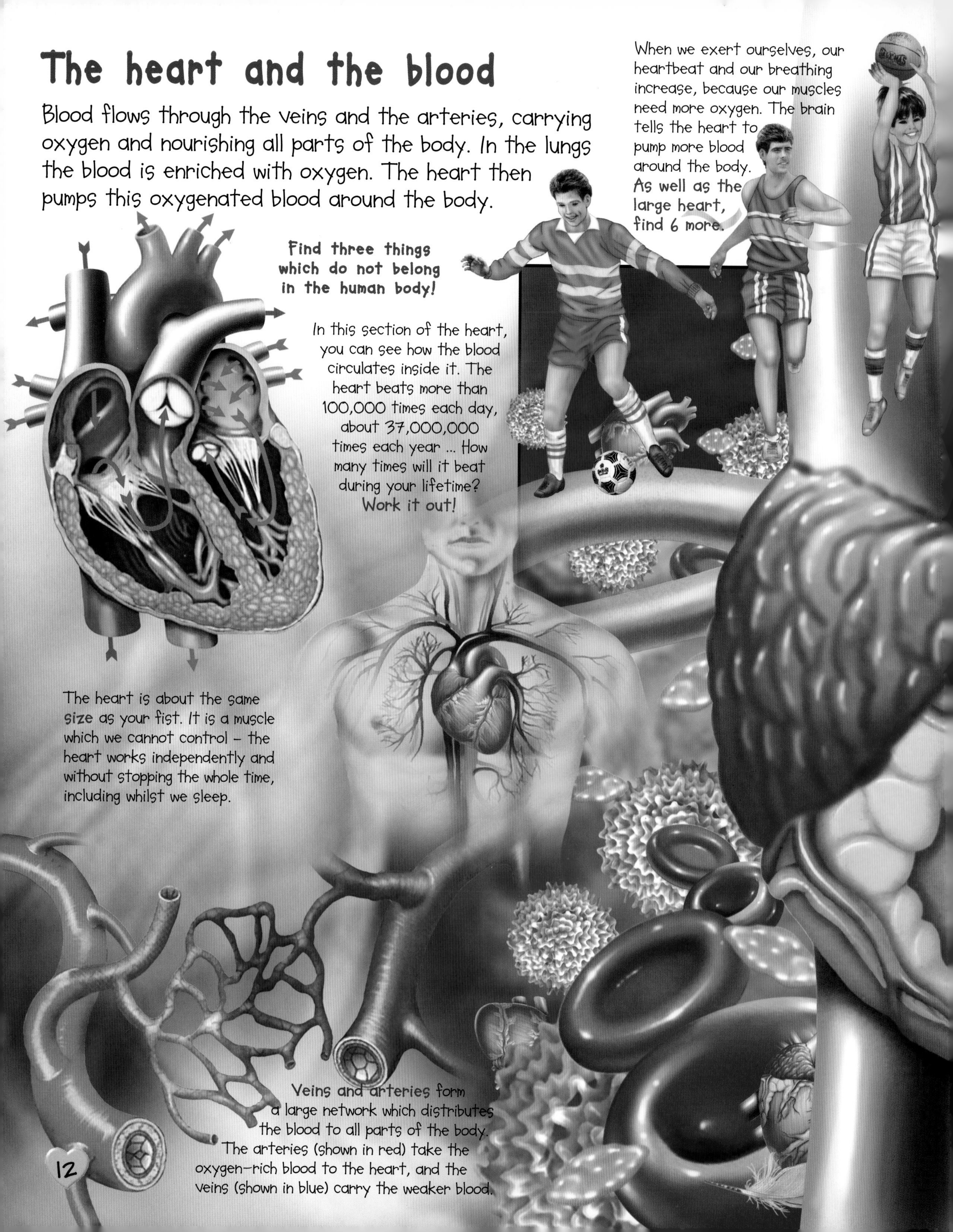

When we exert ourselves, our heartbeat and our breathing increase, because our muscles need more oxygen. The brain tells the heart to pump more blood around the body.

As well as the large heart, find 6 more.

Find three things which do not belong in the human body!

In this section of the heart, you can see how the blood circulates inside it. The heart beats more than 100,000 times each day, about 37,000,000 times each year ... How many times will it beat during your lifetime? Work it out!

The heart is about the same **size** as your fist. It is a muscle which we cannot control – the heart works independently and without stopping the whole time, including whilst we sleep.

Veins and arteries form a large network which distributes the blood to all parts of the body. The arteries (shown in red) take the oxygen-rich blood to the heart, and the veins (shown in blue) carry the weaker blood.

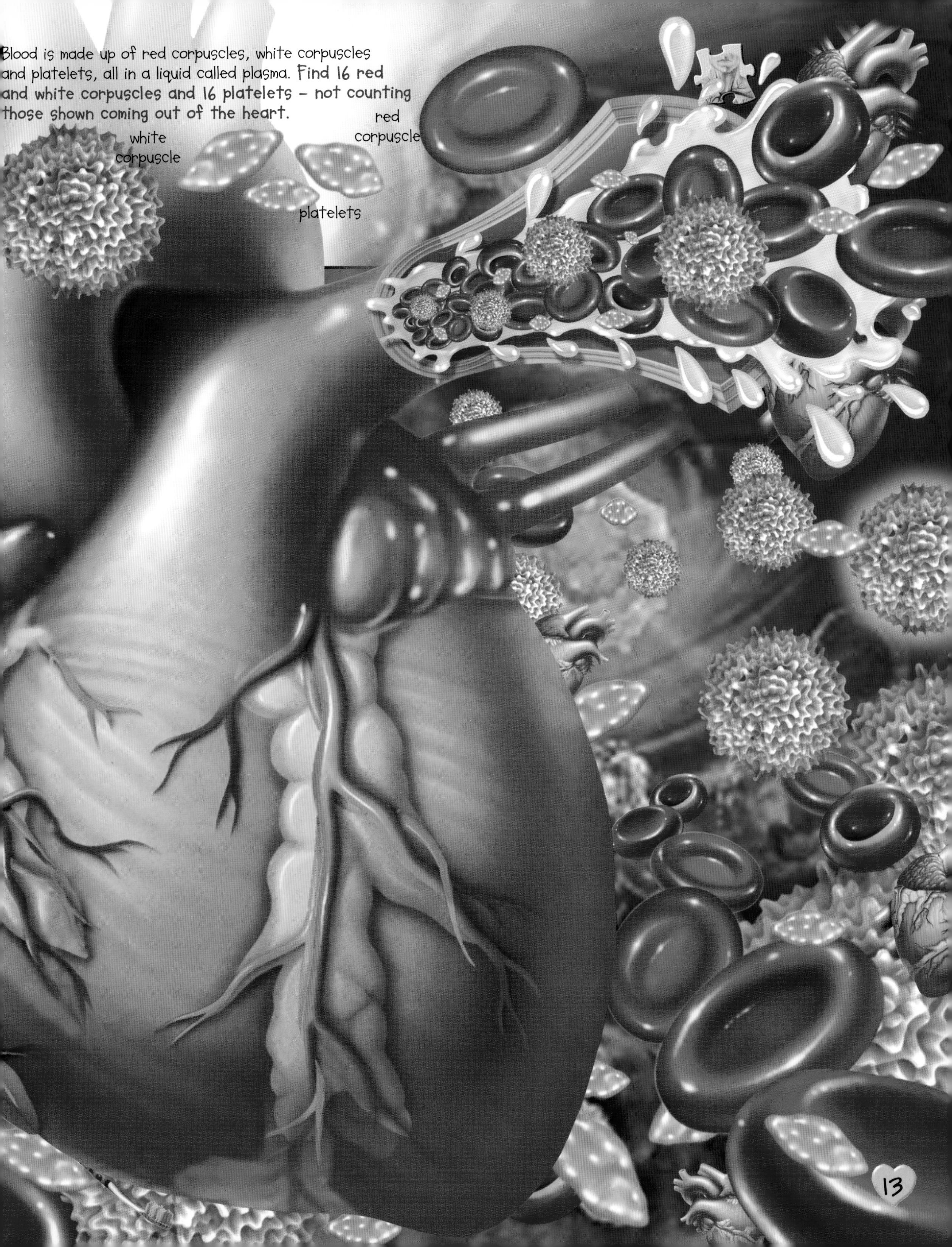
Blood is made up of red corpuscles, white corpuscles and platelets, all in a liquid called plasma. Find 16 red and white corpuscles and 16 platelets – not counting those shown coming out of the heart.
white corpuscle
platelets
red corpuscle

The respiratory system

There are two lungs in the human body. These are situated within the thorax, protected by the ribs. The lungs are very important, because they supply the blood with oxygen, through alveoli – tiny, little tubes which fill up with air

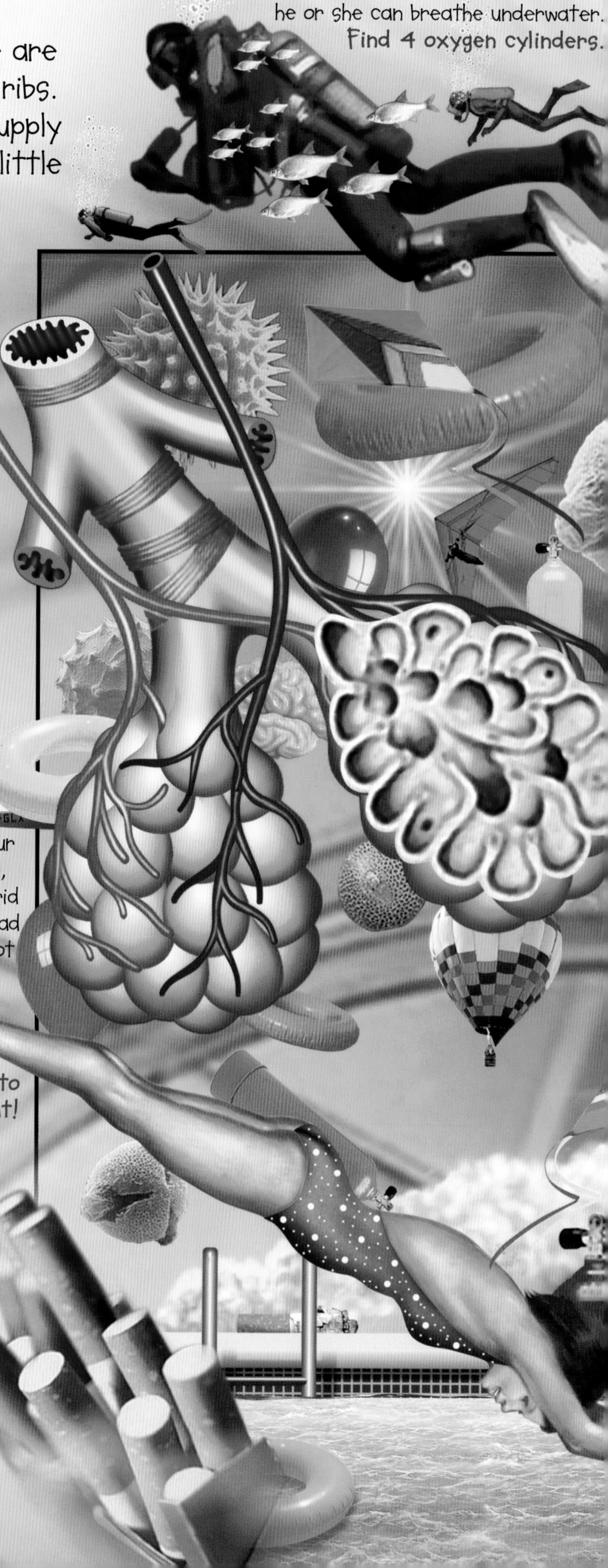

To be able to dive, a person has to carry compressed air, so that he or she can breathe underwater. **Find 4 oxygen cylinders.**

Like the heart, our lungs are working even when we are asleep. **But, if you fall asleep, you will not see 8 things which need air – not for breathing, but to fly!**

Air pollution is a big problem which affects our lungs. **Find 5 clouds of toxic (poisonous) gas.**

Alveoli are tiny, little tubes formed in clusters, like little bunches of grapes. When we breathe in, these fill with air and take oxygen to the blood. **Can you find 9 alveoli?**

If we take water into our lungs, we cannot breathe, and so we cough to get rid of it; but if a person's head is under water, this is not possible. So, that person may suffocate or even drown. **Pick out 8 rubber rings to keep us afloat!**

Smoking is not only dangerous to smokers, but also to those around them.

Cross out 4 stinking cigarette ends!

The oil in very old cars gets burning hot, and produces thick clouds of exhaust fumes.

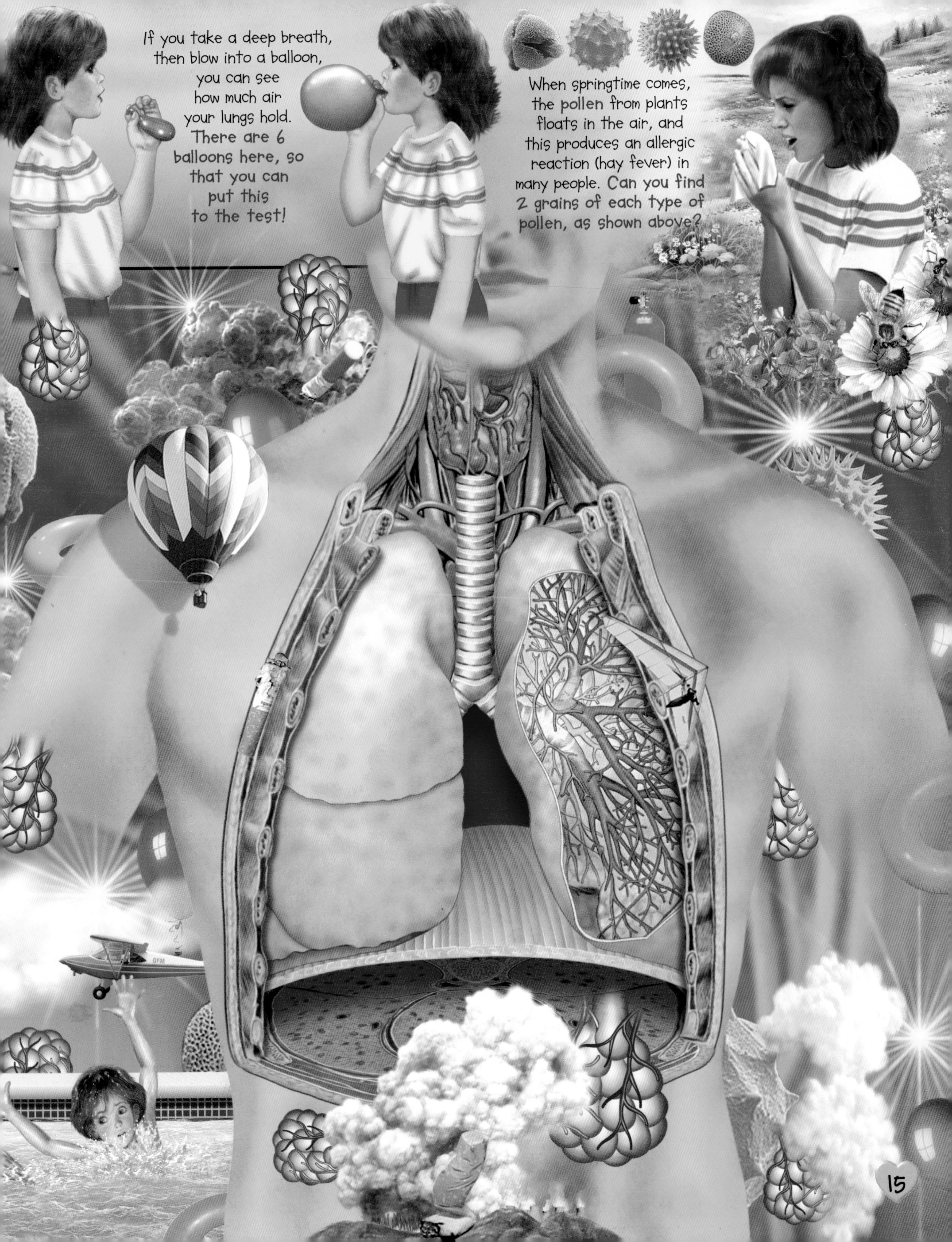
If you take a deep breath, then blow into a balloon, you can see how much air your lungs hold. There are 6 balloons here, so that you can put this to the test!
When springtime comes, the pollen from plants floats in the air, and this produces an allergic reaction (hay fever) in many people. Can you find 2 grains of each type of pollen, as shown above?
GF98

The digestive system

Basically, the digestive system is a channel which starts at the mouth and ends at the anus. Food goes down the oesophagus (food-pipe), then it is ground up in the stomach, before passing into the small intestine where the blood is nourished by proteins from the food. The remainder then passes into the large intestine and anything which is not digested by that time is expelled through the anus.

During digestion, our stomach is very much like a food processor, transforming the food we eat into a sort of watery paste. **Find 5 food processors!**

We have made 4 cakes... but where are they?

A good appetite is a sign that a person is feeling well. But over-eating causes many problems. **For healthy eating, find 8 different types of fruit!**

The **stomach** is vital for the digestion. Here, food is broken down and transformed into tiny little pieces. **This process takes about two hours.**

Too much time sitting on the sofa is not a good idea, especially for young people. Too little exercise, and a person puts on weight. Sport, or even just walking, is good for the heart, as well as helping to control our weight. **Now find 4 foods which contain lots of fat!**

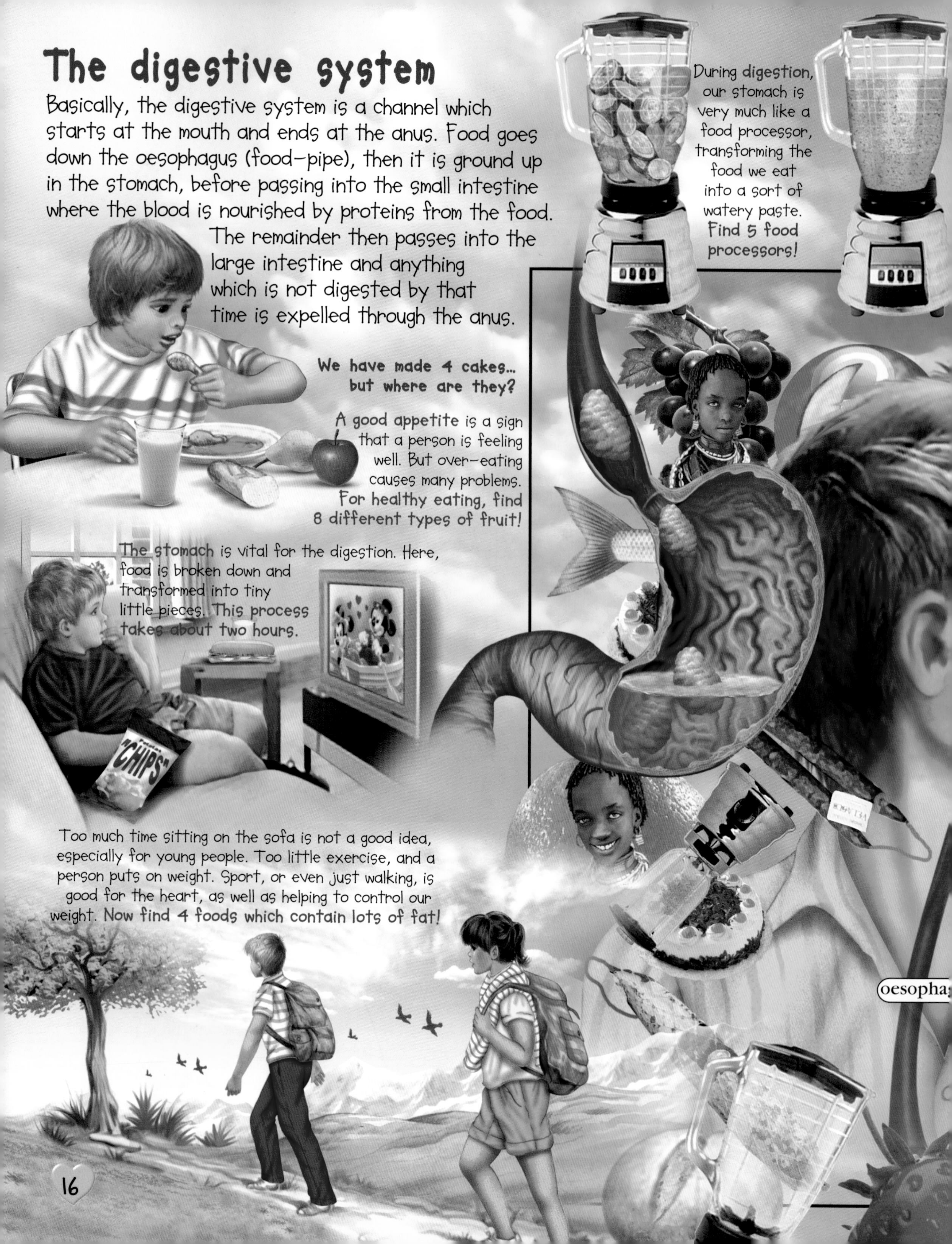

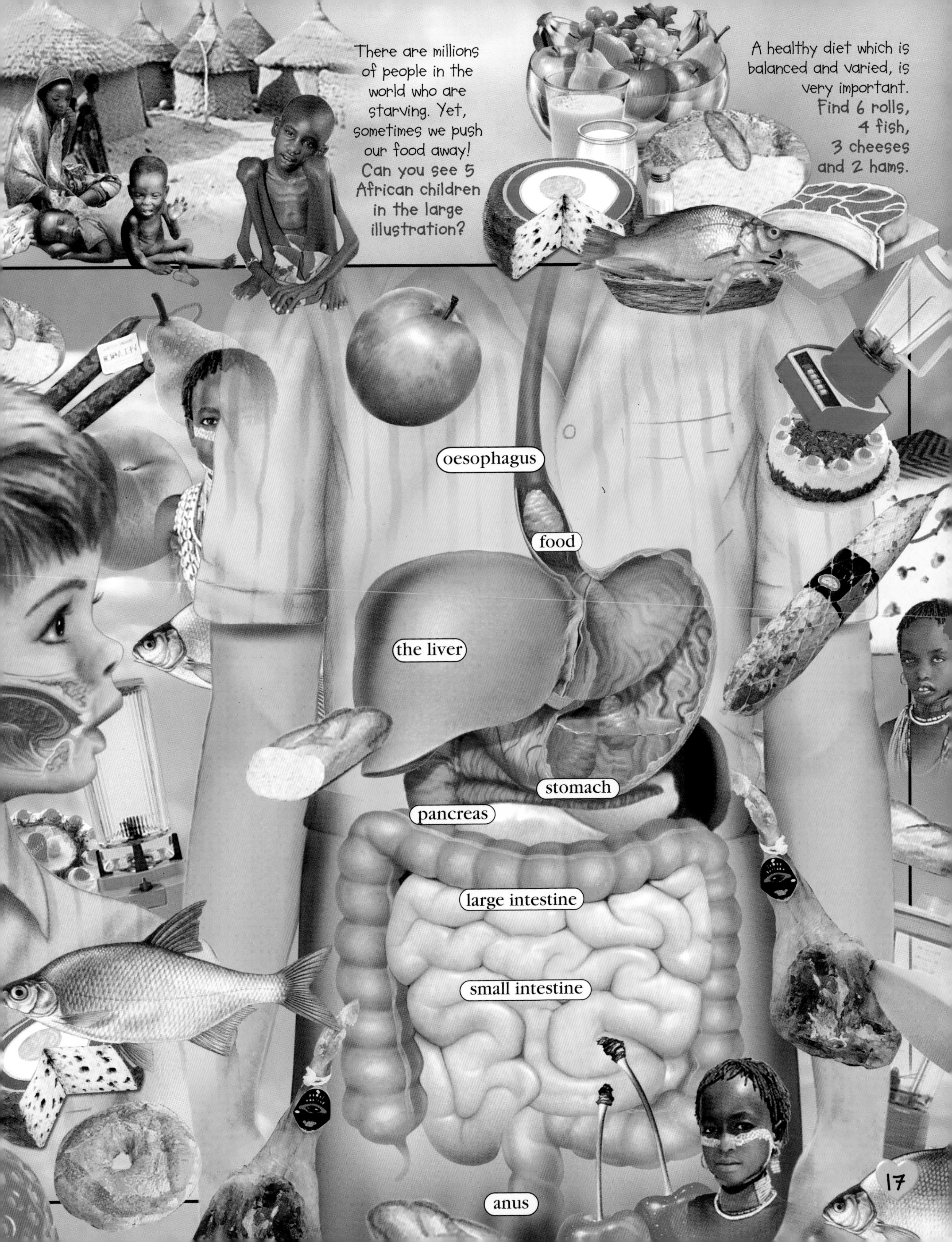
There are millions of people in the world who are starving. Yet, sometimes we push our food away! Can you see 5 African children in the large illustration?
A healthy diet which is balanced and varied, is very important. Find 6 rolls, 4 fish, 3 cheeses and 2 hams.
oesophagus
food
the liver
stomach
pancreas
large intestine
small intestine
anus

The muscles

Whatever movement we make – walking, playing ... even blinking – the body uses muscles. Some move as we wish. Others, like the heart, the muscles in the intestine and the respiratory system move without our knowledge, even when we are asleep.

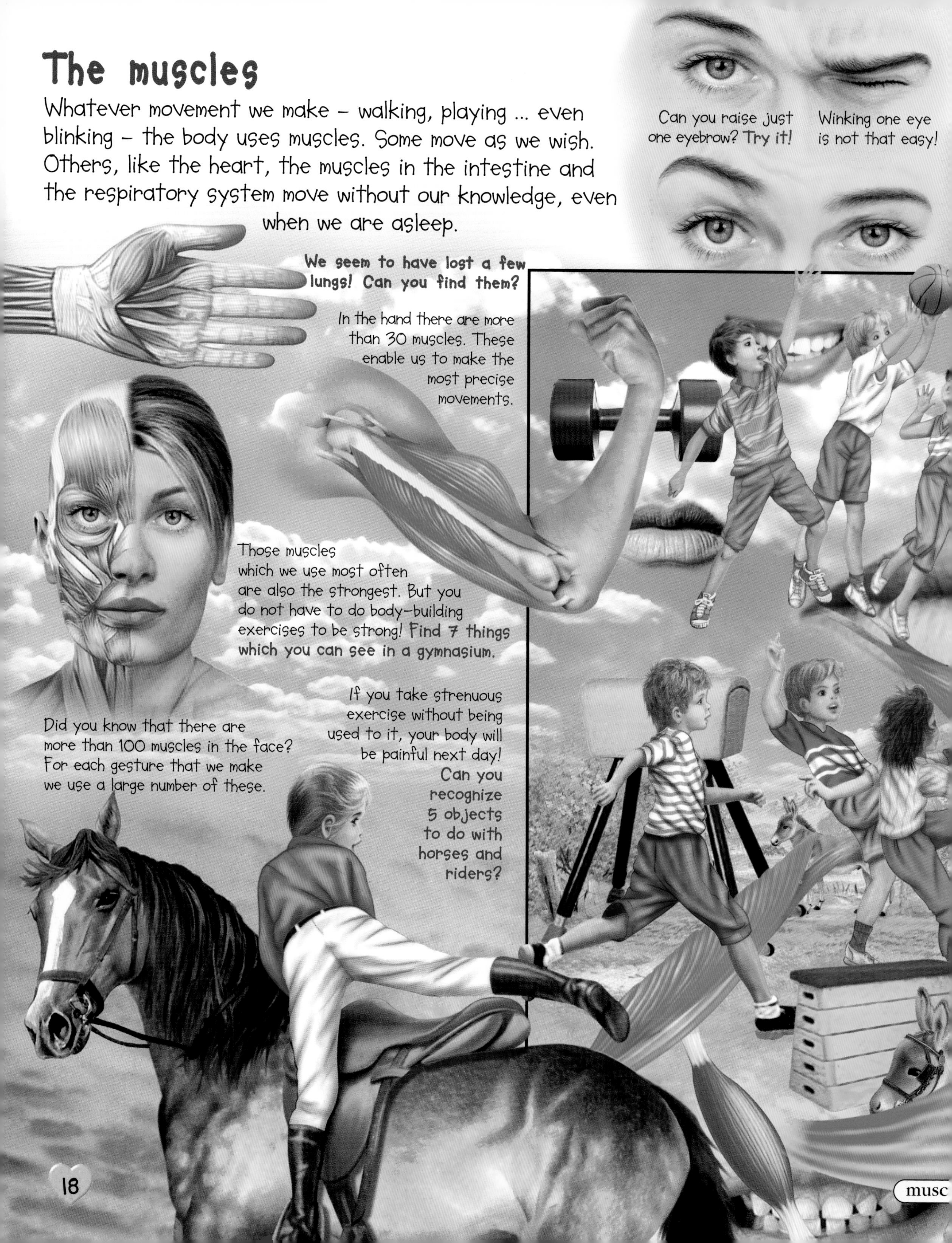

Can you raise just one eyebrow? Try it!

Winking one eye is not that easy!

We seem to have lost a few lungs! Can you find them?

In the hand there are more than 30 muscles. These enable us to make the most precise movements.

Those muscles which we use most often are also the strongest. But you do not have to do body-building exercises to be strong! **Find 7 things which you can see in a gymnasium.**

Did you know that there are more than 100 muscles in the face? For each gesture that we make we use a large number of these.

If you take strenuous exercise without being used to it, your body will be painful next day! **Can you recognize 5 objects to do with horses and riders?**

Did you know that when we smile we use 30 muscles? You won't laugh if you cannot find 7 smiles!
Can you imagine the number of muscles being moved by these children and the donkey? And, can you find 6 more donkeys?
myofibril
protein chain
muscle cells

OUR BONES

There are 260 bones in the human skeleton – 29 in the cranium (skull); 26 in the spinal column; 25 in the rib cage and 64 in the arms and hands. Altogether, the legs and feet have 62 bones. We need to take special care of the bones in our head and in our spinal column.

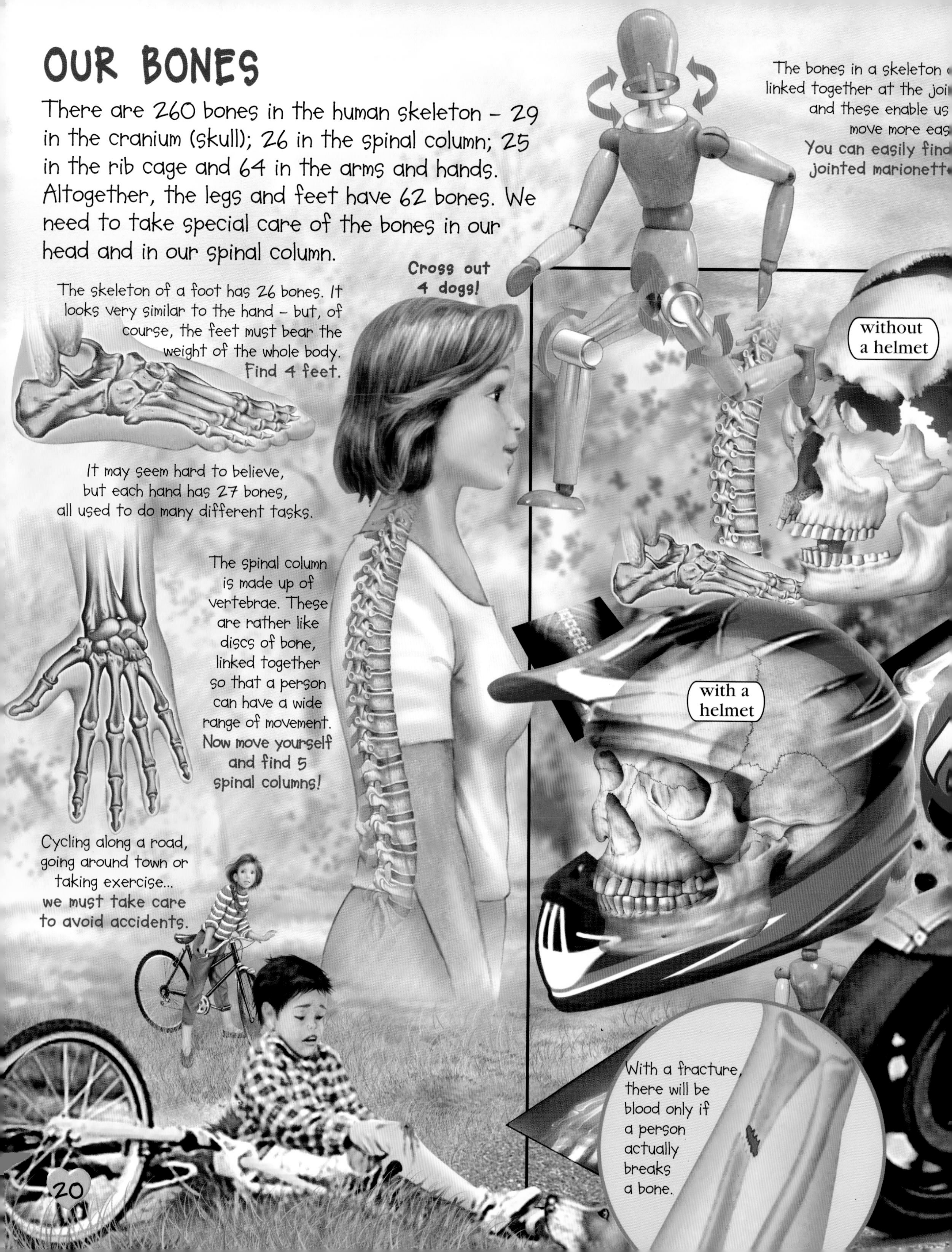

The bones in a skeleton
linked together at the joi
and these enable us
move more eas
You can easily find
jointed marionett

Cross out 4 dogs!

The skeleton of a foot has 26 bones. It looks very similar to the hand – but, of course, the feet must bear the weight of the whole body. Find 4 feet.

It may seem hard to believe, but each hand has 27 bones, all used to do many different tasks.

The spinal column is made up of vertebrae. These are rather like discs of bone, linked together so that a person can have a wide range of movement. Now move yourself and find 5 spinal columns!

Cycling along a road, going around town or taking exercise... **we must take care to avoid accidents.**

With a fracture, there will be blood only if a person actually breaks a bone.

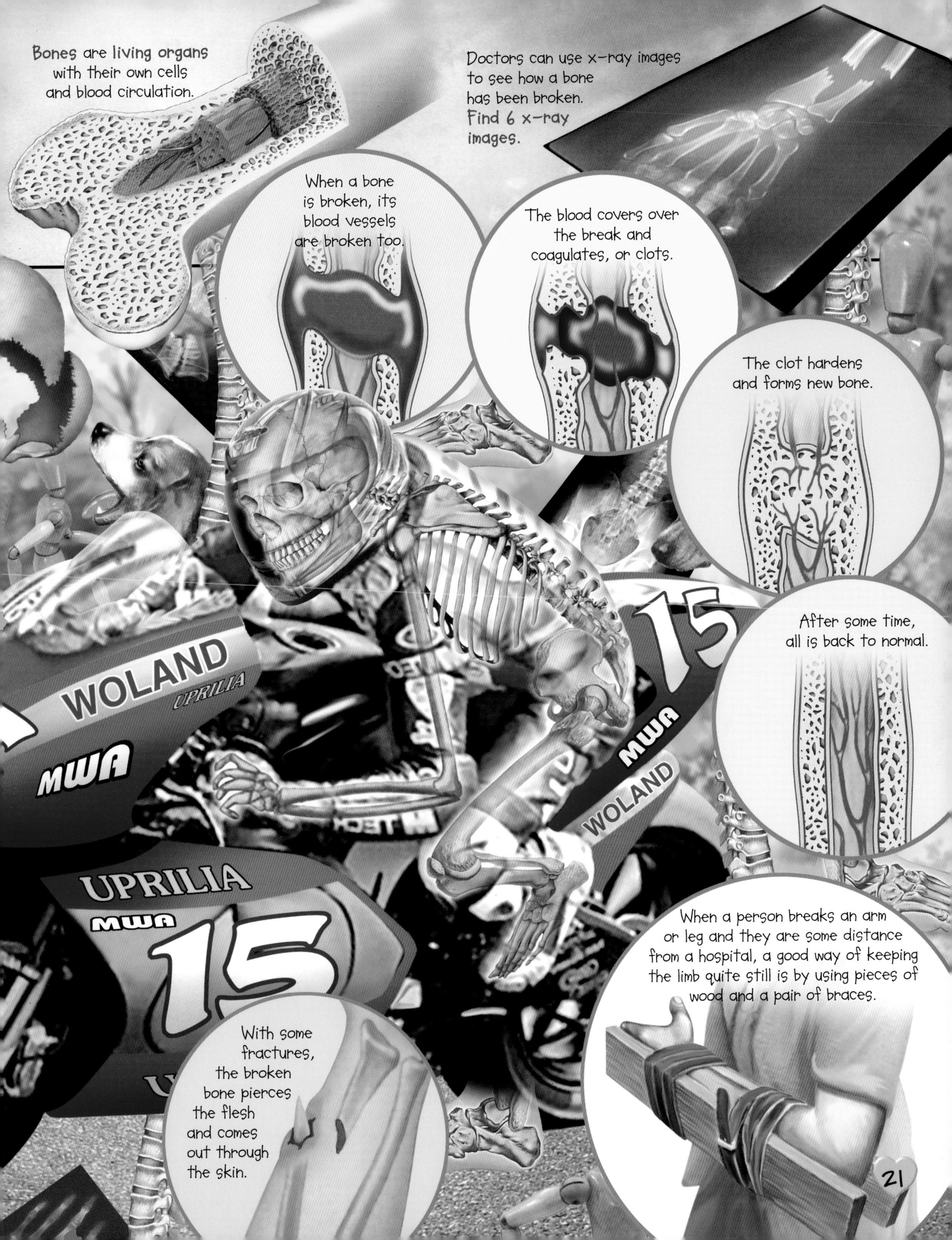

Bones are living organs with their own cells and blood circulation.
Doctors can use x-ray images to see how a bone has been broken.
Find 6 x-ray images.
When a bone is broken, its blood vessels are broken too.
The blood covers over the break and coagulates, or clots.
The clot hardens and forms new bone.
After some time, all is back to normal.
WOLAND
UPRILIA
MWA
15
MWA
WOLAND
UPRILIA
MWA
15
When a person breaks an arm or leg and they are some distance from a hospital, a good way of keeping the limb quite still is by using pieces of wood and a pair of braces.
With some fractures, the broken bone pierces the flesh and comes out through the skin.

Filters in the body

Our kidneys filter our blood and control the chemical balance of the body. The waste is expelled through our urine. The kidneys are vital, because they prevent waste material getting into the blood.

Help! We've lost a heart, a lung, a stomach and a brain. Can you find them?

A healthy liver is necessary for our well-being. For this, we have to avoid eating too much of certain foods.

Too much alcohol seriously affects the liver.

The destruction of the tissues of the liver causes a disease called cirrhosis. Cross out 9 bottles of alcohol!

The work of the kidneys is to filter out harmful substances. It is rather like this butterfly net, attracting the butterflies to go inside it as they flutter through the air. Find 12 butterflies.

The liver collects and stores proteins and sugars, and distributes these according to where they are needed in the body.

Some specially-kept geese are fattened by force-feeding, to make the famous pate de foie gras from their livers. Here, you can find 11 healthy geese!

Thousands of pilgrims gather along the shores of the River Ganges in India. But many illnesses can be passed on through water.

When kidneys fail, a person goes on a dialysis machine and this purifies the blood.
A donated kidney can save a life – but it must be a match for the person receiving it, otherwise the body will reject it.
interior of kidney
kidney
ureter
bladder

The miracle of life

A man and a woman have different reproductive systems. In a female the reproductive cells are the ovules (eggs) and in a male, the spermatozoa. If a sperm meets an ovule, then the sperm can fertilize it and a new life will begin.

Find 7 babies which are already born.

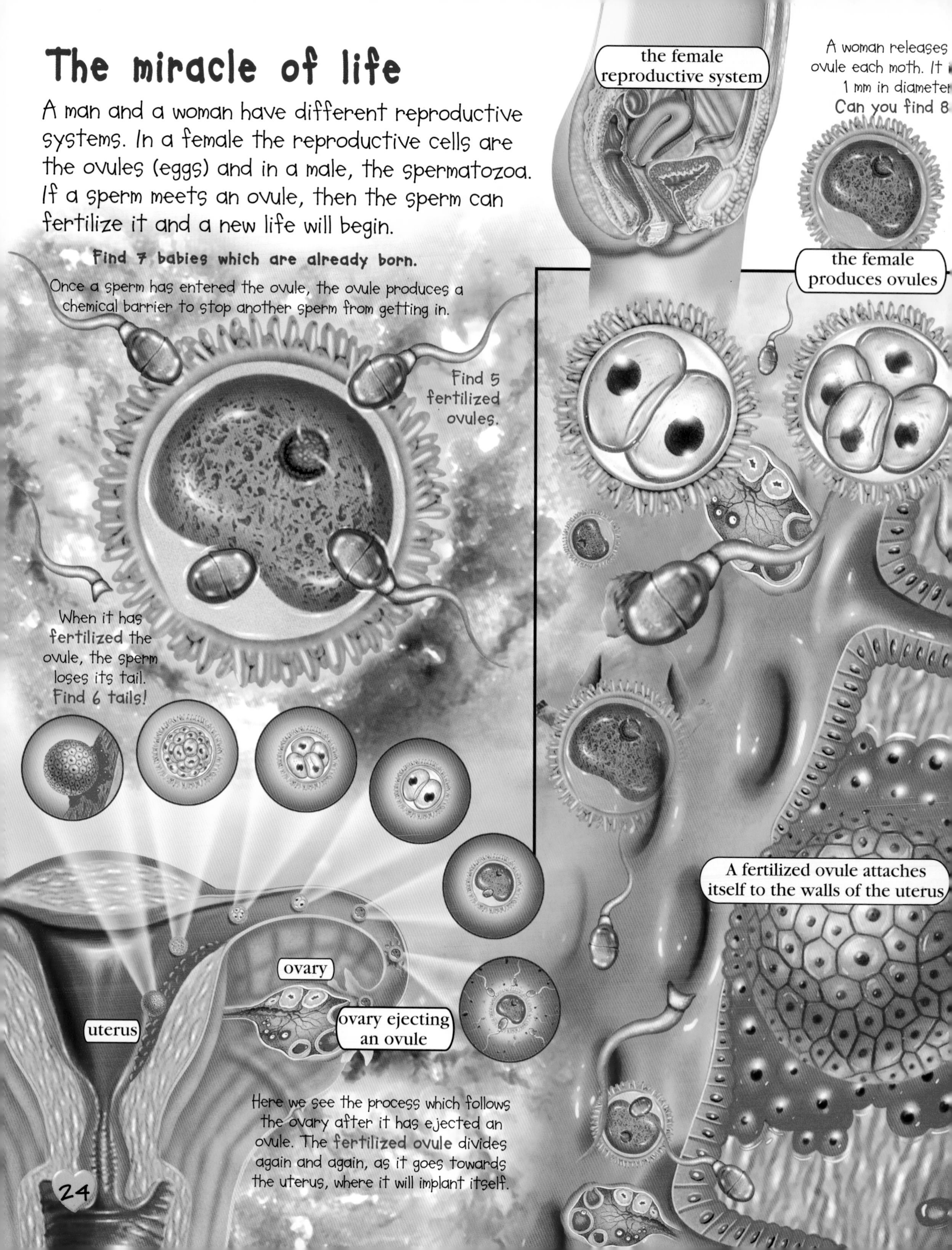

Once a sperm has entered the ovule, the ovule produces a chemical barrier to stop another sperm from getting in.
Find 5 fertilized ovules.
When it has fertilized the ovule, the sperm loses its tail. Find 6 tails!
ovary
uterus
ovary ejecting an ovule
Here we see the process which follows the ovary after it has ejected an ovule. The fertilized ovule divides again and again, as it goes towards the uterus, where it will implant itself.
the female reproductive system
A woman releases
ovule each moth. It
1 mm in diameter
Can you find 8
the female produces ovules
A fertilized ovule attaches itself to the walls of the uterus

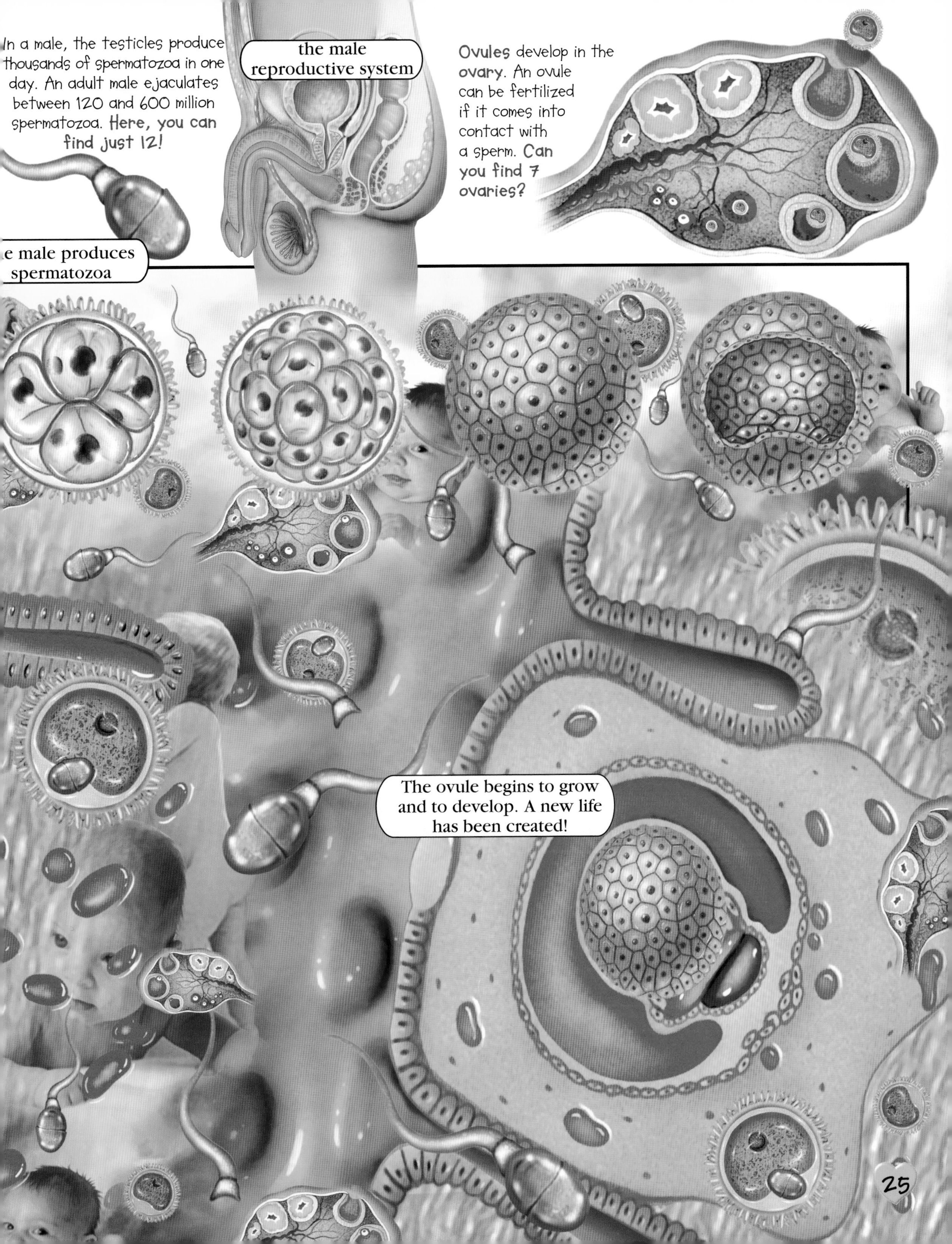
In a male, the testicles produce thousands of spermatozoa in one day. An adult male ejaculates between 120 and 600 million spermatozoa. Here, you can find just 12!
the male reproductive system
Ovules develop in the ovary. An ovule can be fertilized if it comes into contact with a sperm. Can you find 7 ovaries?
e male produces spermatozoa
The ovule begins to grow and to develop. A new life has been created!

Nine amazing months

On these pages, we follow the development of the foetus from five weeks until the time a baby is born – about nine months later.

At seven weeks, the feet and hands have begun to develop.

By five weeks, the head can be seen, also the heart and the spinal column.

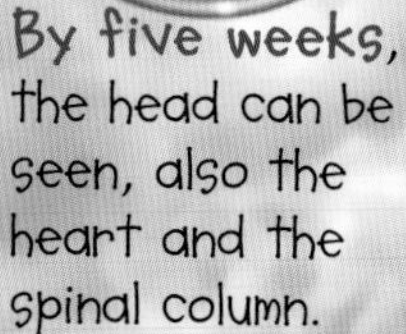

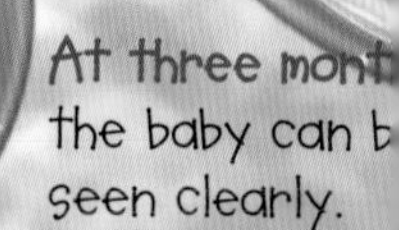

At three mont[hs] the baby can b[e] seen clearly.

Can you find my sister? She is carrying a basket of lettuces!

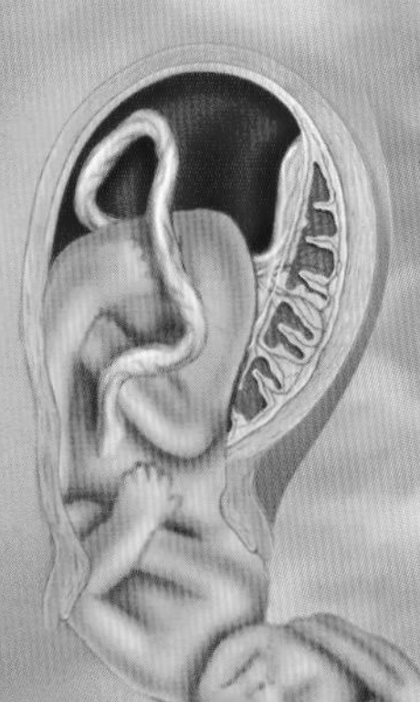

The smallest child is the brother of Jill, the little girl eating an apple. Can you see Jill? Who is her brother?
Jill's Grandma wears spectacles. It's easy to recognize her!

By the time the baby is ready to be born, its head is facing downwards. The mother's birth canal dilates (widens) and contractions from her uterus push the child out. After the birth, a doctor or nurse (midwife) cuts the umbilical cord, through which the baby has received nourishment from the mother as it developed in the uterus.

The doctor then checks that the child and the mother are both all right. Then a nurse cleans the baby.

Now the task of the parents is to feed their child, to see that he or she is educated and to look after it so that he or she grows into a healthy and sensible adult.

By four months
By six months
At nine months, it is time for the baby to be born.
Six children are waiting for Maria, who comes running. Where is she?
Maria's grandfather lives with his daughter, who sells chickens. Can you find Maria's grandfather and her mother?
The daughter of Maria's grandfather has a son, and he is very generous! Can you see him?
Mark wears a pullover. He has a three year old sister and his mother wears a cardigan. Can you find all three?
Mike's sister is feeding the geese. Who is she?
Natalie does not have a bicycle, like Lucy, but she has just bought a green jersey. Can you find both of them?
Have you found everybody? Then find 4 chicks which have escaped!

Hints for good health

Here are some tips for keeping healthy. First, try to avoid unnecessary danger; second, keep yourself and your surroundings clean – and, of course, take exercise, go into the country and have fun!

Your dog must always eat and drink from its own dish. **Find 10 dogs.**

Safety guards on electrical plugs prevent dangerous accidents.

Can you find 3 kittens who have gone on an outing?

A clean body is most important – but having clean hands is absolutely essential, especially before eating. **Now, with clean hands, can you find 9 snacks?**

Small children need lots of care. Many things can injure or choke them. **Pick up 8 pencils from the ground!**

To look after our surroundings, both in our own homes and outside, we must collect up all our litter and put it in a dustbin. As these children know, **there are 5 litter bins to find here.**

When you get anything in your eye, you must remove it with a clean cloth. Then blink hard!
Children must not be left alone in the kitchen, or handle hot cooking utensils or knives. And they must keep away from stoves and ovens!
Find 4 frying-pans 5 knives and 4 gas cylinders

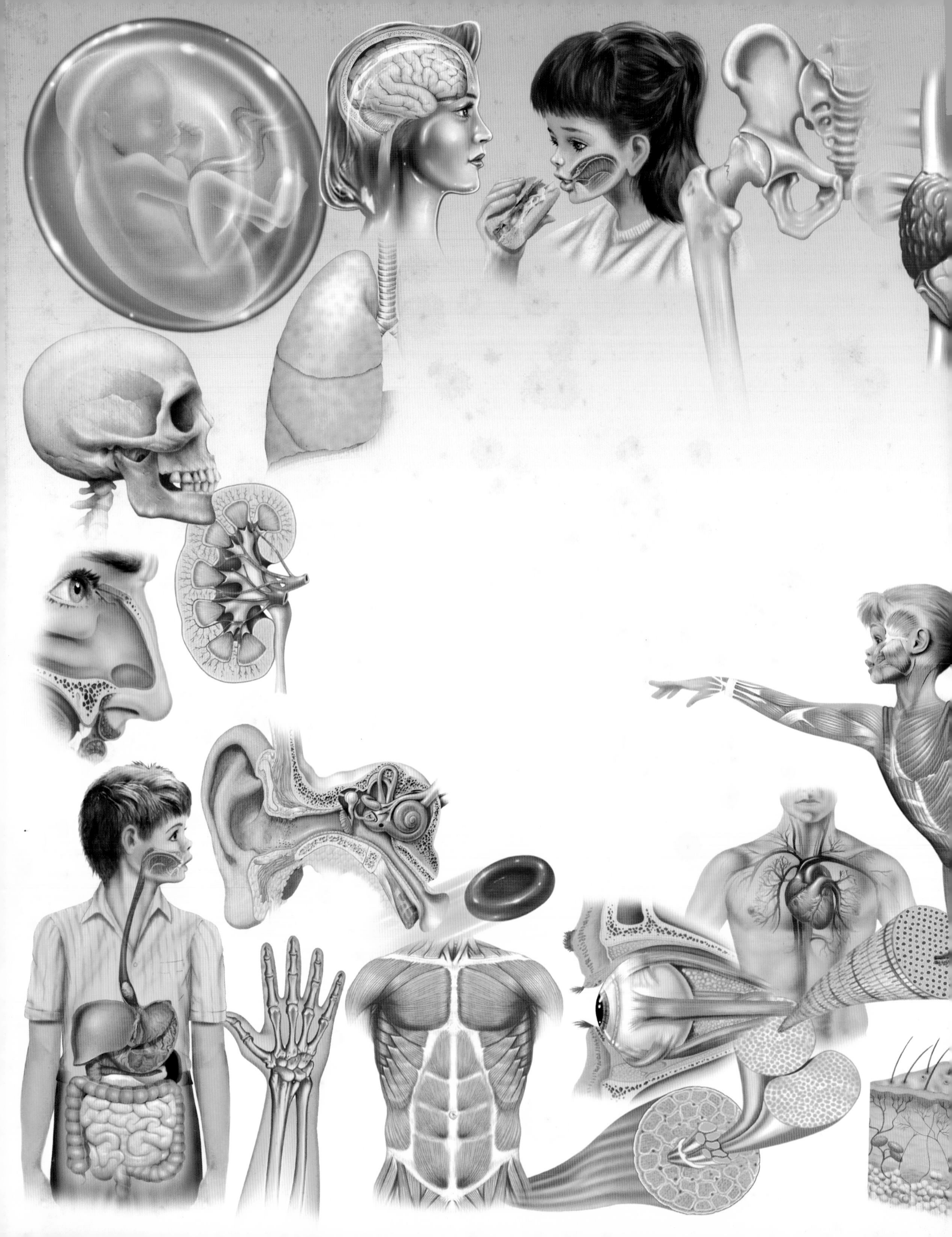